Original title:
Stories from the Shadows

Copyright © 2025 Creative Arts Management OÜ
All rights reserved.

Author: Micah Sterling
ISBN HARDBACK: 978-1-80567-241-8
ISBN PAPERBACK: 978-1-80567-540-2

Narratives from the Night

In the dark, a cat did prance,
Whiskers twitching, seeking chance.
It chased a ghost, quite out of sight,
Who left behind a trail of fright.

A tickled bat flew past my ear,
Squeaking jokes for all to hear.
The moonlight danced on silly dreams,
As laughter echoed through the beams.

Memories in the Mist

In the fog, a rabbit stood,
With a top hat made of wood.
He told a joke to all around,
But only fog could hear the sound.

A squirrel danced in misty glee,
With acorns flying wild and free.
He juggled nuts with nimble paws,
And earned applause from unseen jaws.

Shadows That Speak

In the corner, shadows wiggled,
Chatting softly, laughter giggled.
One claimed it could tell a tale,
Of sock monsters from the vale.

Another whispered, 'Oh, that's lame!',
And recounted a ghostly game.
Where chairs would dance and tables sway,
And knock-knock jokes would steal the day.

The Hidden Chronicles

Beneath the stairs, a mouse did dwell,
With socks and candy, all was well.
It wrote a book of tiny tales,
Of cheese and crumbs, and wind-filled sails.

A party of ants held quite a feast,
With surprises that never ceased.
They boasted of their daring tricks,
The grand parade of snack attack slicks.

Chronicles of the Silent Veil

In the alley, cats plot
With tails flicking, they trot,
Under moonlit, they meet,
Dancing softly on their feet.

A raccoon steals a slice of pie,
With a twinkle in his eye,
He juggles scraps with grace,
Creating chaos in the place.

Bats gossip as they fly,
Daring to spread a sly lie,
They whisper, 'Did you see?'
That squirrel caught a fierce bee!

And in the night, laughter rings,
As shadows wear the best of blings,
Life's a joke beneath the stars,
Even when we slip on jars!

Legends from the Hidden Path

Behind the trees, a legless frog,
Challenges a sleepy dog,
With a ribbit and a wink,
They're plotting mischief, don't you think?

A turtle wearing a crown,
Challenges a rabbit in town,
'Bet you can't outrun my waddle,'
And the rabbit gives a nod to throttle.

In the bushes, two mice conspire,
Building traps with strings of wire,
They giggle at their grand plans,
As they craft tiny, sticky bands.

The night is filled with silly quirks,
As shadows spin their playful works,
In every nook, in every crack,
Laughter echoes through each track!

Fables in the Flickering Dark

A ghost with a fondness for cheese,
Scares the cat with wobbly knees,
'I just want a snack,' he pleads,
Cat rolls her eyes, but he proceeds.

In the corner, old shoes discuss,
Why they're left behind, no fuss,
One claims they danced with a shoehorn,
While another moans of a heart torn.

A lamp winks knowingly at a broom,
'Let's sweep away this gloom,' it zooms,
Together they spin and twirl, oh so bold,
In a flicker of light, their tales unfold.

Every corner has its jesters,
Bringing giggles, not just testers,
In the dark, let laughter spark,
As we dance through the playful park!

Reflections in Dim Light

Underneath the old park bench,
A spider spins with flair, a wrench,
Inviting ants to see her show,
But they scurry fast, oh no, oh no!

Behind the bushes, a chipmunk grins,
Holding secrets of wild, funny wins,
'The raccoon tried to play a prank,
But fell in the pond and sank!'

A forgotten sock finds its friend,
In a laugh, they start to blend,
'What's life without a little fun?'
They bounce around, bright as the sun.

In the glow of the fading light,
Shadows dance, such a silly sight,
Laughter drifts on the cool night air,
In every corner, joy is everywhere!

Undercurrents of the Unwritten

In the attic, dust bunnies dance,
They plot with old shoes for a chance.
A cat on the windowsill spies,
The chaos of unknown allies.

A ghost plays chess with a rusty chair,
As socks embark on a secret affair.
They laugh and giggle, what a sight,
In the realm of not quite right.

Old books open, pages fly,
A fairy tale grows legs to try.
The ink spills secrets on the floor,
While knickknacks join in for more.

In this world where whispers creep,
Even the shadows have a leap.
You'd think it's madness, yet it's fun,
When the unwritten tales have begun.

Light on the Frayed Edges.

A button rolls under the bed,
It gathers tales, as if well-read.
With loose threads spinning wild and free,
A patchwork quilt of jubilee.

On frayed edges, laughter's found,
As mismatched socks spin round and round.
A teddy bear, with tales so bold,
Spills beans on adventures untold.

A lamp flickers, but winks just right,
Illuminating the quirky night.
The shadows giggle, light on their toes,
As the mischief in every corner grows.

In corners where dust bunnies roll,
Lies the laughter of a jolly soul.
Fun hides where you least expect,
In the frayed edges we often neglect.

Whispers Beneath the Moonlight

The moon grins bright, a mischievous soul,
While crickets perform, playing their role.
Bats tell jokes in a fluttering flight,
As owls hoot tales that tickle the night.

A mischievous breeze swoops low and sways,
Dancing with shadows, in playful ways.
Ghosts sip tea on the garden swing,
Sharing gossip of a silly fling.

A squirrel with acorns throws a grand feast,
For raccoons and fireflies, scattered at least.
They chatter and giggle beneath starry skies,
In the moon's soft glow, where silliness lies.

Whispers drift on the cool night air,
Collecting chuckles from everywhere.
In this realm where the laughter's in bloom,
The night is alive with the joy of the loom.

Echoes in the Gloom

In a cupboard, echoes tap dance,
A spoon and a cup share a farce and a chance.
The shadows giggle as they collide,
In the corners where jokes like to hide.

A lone lightbulb flickers in tune,
With mischief brewing beneath the moon.
A lizard debates with a wayward shoe,
While the floorboards chuckle, joining the crew.

In nooks and crannies where dust motes trot,
Stories bloom, silly and hot.
As the gloom grows thicker, the fun stays bright,
In the echoes of laughter that dance through the night.

So tiptoe lightly through the chtashed air,
You might find fables with vibrant flair.
For in shadows, humor takes flight,
Making the mundane a true delight.

Phantom Echoes of Time

In a cupboard, a ghostly sock,
Wanders free, oh what a shock!
It tells of days when it could dance,
With a partner—no second chance.

Underneath the bed, an old lunch bin,
Holds tales of peanut butter and grin.
Every bite was a leap of fate,
Moldy stories that wouldn't wait.

A specter's laugh from the attic above,
Sings of love played out like a glove.
With every creak, there's a new twist,
Too funny to be left off the list.

Beneath the stairs, a broom takes flight,
In the moonlight, it joins the night.
Whirling past, with ghosts in tow,
Making messes as they go.

Wandering in the Twilight

A cat in a hat, what a sight,
Prancing through the soft twilight.
He tells the tales of all he's seen,
Of mice in chairs where they have been.

A whispered giggle from the fence,
Invisible friends with much pretense.
They share their giggles, full of charm,
With silly antics that cause alarm.

A plant in the window, gossiping loud,
Of a squirrel who thought he was proud.
Chasing dreams through the garden green,
While dodging shoes that hit the scene.

And then there's a broom that's tired of dust,
Wishing for freedom, it means they must.
To wander the streets and do a little dance,
In the soft twilight, they take a chance.

Lost in the Fog

A traveler stumbles, lost in the haze,
With a map upside down, in a daze.
"Is that a tree or a sheep?" he will shout,
As the fog giggles softly, all about.

He trips on a log, looking for signs,
Mistakes a raccoon for a pair of fines.
"Maybe the road is just being shy,
Or playing hide and seek, oh my!"

Phantoms of the Forgotten

In an old house, ghosts rehearse their play,
One forgot his line, and wandered away.
The chandelier shakes with a chuckling sound,
As they giggle and jump all around.

A phantom once tried to scare with a whack,
But the broomstick slipped and sent him back.
"Oops! Was that a scare? I meant 'hello!'"
Laughter echoes in the moon's soft glow.

Tales from the Depths

Under the waves where the jellyfish dance,
A fish cracked a joke, it led to romance!
"Why did the crab never share his food?"
"Because he was shellfish, oh how rude!"

An octopus laughed, said with glee,
"I can juggle eight things, come try with me!"
The seaweed swayed to the rhythm so fine,
As the fish told tall tales over brine.

Reverberations of the Unseen

In the attic, the whispers are quite a delight,
They gossip and giggle through the long night.
"Did you hear the rumor? The cat has a plot!"
"Oh please, she just wants to nap a whole lot!"

A sock floats by, on its own little spree,
"What's next?" it yells, "A dance party for me!"
The echoing chuckles fill up the room,
As shadows join in, to escape from the gloom.

The Veil Between

In the corner, ghosts with style,
Hiding secrets, flashing a smile.
Jeans and jackets, they've got flair,
Dancing shadows without a care.

They toss confetti made of dust,
Declaring life is a must.
Whispers saying, 'We're alive!'
Playing tricks, while shadows thrive.

Lost Legends in the Dusk

Here in twilight, gnomes convene,
Stealing snacks, a comical scene.
Telling tales of ancient lore,
While munching chips they can't ignore.

They argue fiercely, who was brave,
While dancing on a miniature wave.
With every laugh, the tales grow tall,
Each puff of laughter breaks the wall.

Stories Chiseled in Darkness

Figures chiseled with a grin,
Bouncing tales like pinballs, in.
Chasing dreams in the night air,
Making mischief, taking care.

A friendly ghost with a top hat,
Cracks a joke, a playful spat.
When the sun sets, they take their stand,
Whirling whispers, a funny band.

Whispers Linger in the Background

In the backdrop, shadows wink,
Spinning yarns, on the brink.
Witty banter, a daily treat,
Twirling tales with nimble feet.

They play charades behind the door,
Rolling laughter on the floor.
With every giggle, tales unfold,
In the dark, their antics bold.

Masks of the Forgotten

In a town where socks often flee,
A pot-bellied man sips his tea.
His hat tells tales of places wide,
While old shoes dance, they won't abide.

A cat with a penchant for jazz,
Plays the trumpet, oh what a fizz!
The furniture giggles, a grand parade,
With every chair, a serenade.

The clock ticks tales of merry pranks,
While gnomes play cards and toast with flanks.
In daylight, they whisper, at night they croon,
The moon joins in, they dance till noon.

When shadows stretch and whispers blend,
You'll find a raccoon who's made a friend.
Together they plot in the twilight glow,
A pillow fight with a sleeping crow.

Secrets in the Stillness

In the attic, dust bunnies conspire,
To tell of socks lost in the fire.
A broom takes flight, a daring soar,
Chasing the cat that's hiding more.

Crickets sing with a cheeky flair,
While curtains sway without a care.
Grandma's rocking chair spins a tale,
Of ships that sailed beyond the pale.

A teapot laughs, almost in glee,
As it whispers secrets, just like me.
The shadows wiggle, daringly bold,
Unraveling wonders yet to be told.

The grandfather clock reveals its plot,
Ticking time to a dance, oh so hot!
In stillness, laughter spills like wine,
For every quiet, there's a punchline.

Murmurs of the Abandoned

In a ghost town where whispers roam,
A pair of shoes still wait for home.
Old lampposts giggle, shadows tease,
As they play tag with the autumn breeze.

A swing sways gently, no child in sight,
Yet sings to the moon, a joyful night.
The weathered fence leans in to share,
Tall tales of love and a tiny bear.

Paint peels back, revealing dreams,
Muffins argue about buttered seams.
Windows wink with mischievous glee,
In every crack, there's a memory spree.

The past holds court, it's a laugh fest,
As echoes of joy refuse to rest.
With every sigh, the old walls cheer,
For laughter lives, even when it's near.

Shadows that Speak

In the park where shadows convene,
A merry band of old folks preen.
With upturned hats and whispers bright,
They plot their antics under the moonlight.

A bench tells tales of lovers lost,
While squirrels debate what's worth the cost.
The fountain giggles, splashes around,
As pigeons conspire in silent sound.

The moon joins in with a silvery grin,
While shadows gather, their dance begins.
Each flicker tells a jolly jest,
In the laughter, you'll find your quest.

As night unfolds, the stories whirl,
With every turn, a twist, a twirl.
In darkness, light finds a way to peek,
A choir of giggles, from shadows that speak.

Subtle Shades of Memory

In a corner, dust bunnies play,
They dance with the socks that ran away.
A forgotten shoe sings a comedic tune,
As shadows waltz by the light of the moon.

The cat naps on tales of yesterday,
While the chair recalls the games we'd play.
A mismatched sock holds secrets from time,
Whispers of laughter, all in good rhyme.

Lost marbles chat with the old tin can,
Discussing the antics of the family clan.
A quirky clock ticks with a wink and a nod,
Counting the giggles, giving a prod.

Echoes of voices, they mumble and tease,
The shadows conspire, if you please.
As the curtains flutter, secrets unfold,
In this playful realm where memories are sold.

Murmurs in the Half-Light

In the kitchen, pots and pans laugh loud,
They clatter and sing, a clumsy crowd.
Flour on noses, a chef's little prank,
The ghosts of dinner bicker on the plank.

Whispers of butter slide down like a dream,
As shadows collaborate in a buttery scheme.
A rolling pin chortles, a spatula grins,
In the half-light, the fun always begins.

Spices gossip in jars upon shelves,
Tales of the dinners when we cooked ourselves.
While the fridge hums a soft serenade,
The leftovers chuckle, they're not afraid.

Beneath the table, a crumb-saga swells,
With stories of feasts that nobody tells.
In the corners, the shadows join in the fun,
A simple meal becomes a race, a run.

The Silent Archive

Among the books, the dust holds a grin,
Each page a chuckle, a hoot from within.
The ink spills whispers of laughter and jest,
As characters frolic, absently blessed.

A tale about socks that never match,
Detours in life that scratch and scratch.
The stories unfold on the spine's gentle bend,
With puns and quips, they just never end.

A parrot from a fairy tale quips with delight,
While a knight on a taco guards his plight.
The shadows converse as the lamp flickers bright,
In this placid world, there's always a light.

Laughter erupts from the corners and cracks,
As books whisper secrets, the joy never lacks.
In this silent space, a party takes flight,
With shadows and stories, a whimsical night.

Unillumined Fables

In the nooks where the shadows feel bold,
Lie fables untold, with laughter retold.
The old broom chuckles, its bristles a mess,
As whispers of gnomes spark joyous distress.

A cat with a grin sings lullabies sweet,
To the dust motes that dance on nimble feet.
The old chair groans with tales of great fun,
When the kids were wild, and laughter begun.

Behind the curtains, a squirrel takes note,
Writing out tales of the spy in the coat.
A shadow of mischief hangs by the wall,
As echoes of giggles bloom and enthrall.

In the haze of twilight, secrets ignite,
The unlit fables come alive each night.
With wit in their hearts and a twinkle in eyes,
Every shadow tells tales, of mischief and surprise.

Luminescence in the Gloom

In a world where snails wear hats,
And cats play cards with their spats,
The shadows chuckle and tease,
As they dance in light with such ease.

A ghost who wants to bake a pie,
But burns it with a spooky sigh,
Says, "I guess I'll haunt the bake sale!"
With silly jokes, he'll surely prevail!

The whispers sing with glee and cheer,
As shadows trip on their own sheer,
They drop their woes and jump with glee,
Creating joy in mystery.

A wiggly worm in a tutu pranced,
Said to the bugs, "Come on, let's dance!"
In the dim light, all creatures grin,
Embracing merriment from within.

Insights from the Edge of Darkness

A shadow shakes its silly form,
In the dark, it's quite the norm,
To have a laugh at silly sights,
Like bats who think they're taking flights.

A spider knitting webs for fun,
Wants to make a hat for a pun,
But weaves a scarf instead, oh dear!
She spins her tales while shedding cheer.

In corners where the ghouls convene,
They play chess with beans, quite obscene,
Each move a giggle, who will win?
The game gets loud; let the fun begin!

A raccoon dons a pirate hat,
And says to friends, "Look at that!"
They raid the garbage, causing a scene,
With laughter echoing in between.

Forgotten Footsteps

Footsteps echo in a silly tune,
Where shadows gather and dance by the moon,
A poltergeist cases out a prank,
As it hops upon the neighbor's shank.

The lost shoes giggle on the floor,
One's a slipper, the other's a chore,
They twirl and twist in a shoe ballet,
Catching all tangled socks at play.

A sneaky shadow steals the show,
With jokes about a pig named Joe,
His punchlines flop in a friendly way,
Yet the laughter echoes, brightens the day.

In corners where the quirks reside,
They throw a feast with rabbit pride,
Forgotten footsteps, never alone,
In laughter's grip, they find their home.

The Veil of Stern Silence

Beneath a veil of solemn play,
The shadows whisper jokes all day,
A grumpy ghost with a frown so deep,
    Cackles at secrets he can't keep.

A silence filled with absurd delight,
As shadows clash in a mock fight,
One says, "I'm an elephant!" from below,
While another insists, "No, you're a crow!"

The serious beans in their nightly brawl,
Turned rebels with ketchup at their call,
They splash and giggle, free from care,
    Creating laughter in the dark air.

A statue winks as the moon shines bright,
    Conspiring with shadows for a night,
Together they craft the silliest tales,
    As the veil of silence happily fails.

Whispers of the Unseen

In corners dim where laughter hides,
A sock escapes, it giggles, bides.
The cat conspirators patter near,
With tails like tales, they spin in cheer.

A ghost with glasses reads a book,
While shadows dance, each playful nook.
They tease the light, they play amok,
In whimsical plots, they steal the clock.

Behind the curtain, peeks a sprite,
Accidentally stirs a dusty light.
His jester cap, too big, falls down,
He mumbles jokes, wears laughter's crown.

A mirror grins from wall to wall,
Reflecting tricks that twist and sprawl.
In quiet rooms where whispers swell,
The unseen jesters share their spell.

Echoes in the Gloom

In haunted halls where echoes cling,
The walls all chuckle, seem to sing.
A creaky door, a sigh, a squawk,
Turns every step to goofy walk.

A lantern flickers, shadows play,
As batty bats make light of day.
With tiny hats, they fly in grace,
Turning gloom into a merry chase.

A broomstick rides a phantom beast,
Upon a quest for midnight feast.
They joke of ghosts who lost their hue,
In such a dark, they laugh anew.

The curtains sway like dancers bold,
Each echo tells a tale retold.
With giggles and grins, they fill the gloom,
A carnival of fun in every room.

Tales Beneath the Moonlight

Beneath the moon, a raccoon grins,
He tells of cheese and daring wins.
The owls hoot tales with knowing eyes,
While fireflies twinkle as wise guys.

A frog in boots sings songs of woe,
Until the crickets steal the show.
With leaps and jumps, they take the stage,
While shadows cheer, they all engage.

A playful breeze begins to spin,
It carries laughter deep within.
With haunted giggles in the night,
The moonlight joins in, shining bright.

Thus tales unfold in starlit grace,
With every creature taking place.
The whispers dance, the night runs free,
In joyous rapture, harmony.

Secrets Wrapped in Twilight

As twilight wraps the world in dreams,
The cheeky gnomes plot silly schemes.
They hide in plants, they giggle low,
Sharing jokes that make the day glow.

A talking tree shares secrets wide,
With leaves that whisper, side to side.
Each branch a joke, each root a tale,
Of mischief done and fun without fail.

The stars peek down with twinkling eyes,
They chuckle softly, know the wise.
While owls with monocles declare,
That humor's found in every air.

As shadows frolic, twirling bold,
The twilight glimmers with joy untold.
In secrets kept, the laughter grows,
Where every chime of night bestows.

Features of the Fallen

Once a hero with a flair,
Now a sock without a pair.
Fallen off from grace so grand,
Now I just grow ferns on land.

Lofty dreams turned to lemon meringue,
With silly dances and a silly twang.
A king of naps in my fuzzy bed,
Rusty hopes that I once fed.

Wires crossed in my grand design,
Now I wear my shoes askew, divine.
Once I soared like a kite in flight,
Now I'm stuck on this couch tonight.

So raise a toast to fallen pride,
With laughter echoing far and wide.
For it's not the fall that brings the pain,
But the antics that dance in the brain.

Revelations in the Gloom

In a corner where shadows creep,
Lurks a cat that snores in sleep.
Cuppa tea spills on my old sock,
As I ponder time on the ticking clock.

A ghostly laugh from the empty chair,
Turns to hiccups in the frosty air.
Misplaced keys giggle from the floor,
Unlocking laughter behind each door.

Banana peels and eerie sounds,
Whispers of mischief in the bounds.
A sock puppet claims it's a sage,
While I'm trying to find my rage.

In this gloom, we dance and twirl,
With a jig from the ghostly girl.
Who knew the dark could bring such fun?
A comedy act when the day is done.

Shadows Hide the Heart

Under a blanket, a story lies,
Of misguided dreams and sneaky spies.
A rogue squirrel with a treasure trove,
In the attic where dust bunnies rove.

Heart-shaped chocolates in a shoe,
Once sweet gestures, now askew.
Whispers from the light, divine,
"What did you eat? That's the sign!"

Behind the curtain, the shadows play,
As the moons do the tango, sway.
A tickle here, a light poke there,
When darkness laughs, we can only stare.

So let's embrace the ghostly games,
With shadow puppets and funny names.
In this heart, where secrets roam,
We'll find the joy that feels like home.

Timeless Echoes

In the attic of forgotten lore,
Echoes chuckle behind the door.
Tickle the dust with tales so old,
Of socks and spoons that gleam like gold.

Once was a hero, now just a chair,
Worn-out seats with stories to share.
A phantom wiggles in a sock drawer,
Delighting in all the tales of yore.

From giggles that resonate round the bend,
To whispers that tease in the dark, my friend.
A feathered hat and a crooked grin,
Holding onto the silliness within.

Through timeless whispers and funny ways,
Echoes of laughter greet the days.
Join the dance of the unseen crew,
For every shadow has a joke or two.

Tales of the Unseen

In a closet, socks have a chat,
Wandering whiskers debate the cat.
When humans are gone, they dance and they sing,
Life's a party without a boring thing.

Beneath the bed, a rogue shoe awaits,
Prankster spirits set up their plates.
They nibble on crumbs that lovers once left,
In their world, there's never a theft.

A brave little mouse wears a paper crown,
Guiding lost marbles all over town.
With each tiny squeak, they raise a cheer,
For the tiniest creatures have nothing to fear.

So when night falls and you dim the light,
Remember the jests that take playful flight.
For in shadows and corners, the silly reside,
Crafting laughter and tales, their tricks never hide.

Secrets in the Twilight

The toaster whispers, 'Pop goes the bread!'
While the coffee pot schemes, 'Who goes to bed?'
Cupcakes in secret, they plan a parade,
With frosting and sprinkles, they'll not be delayed.

Chairs argue over who gets to seat,
As the lamps flicker with giggles, so sweet.
Mice in tuxedos hold a formal dance,
While dust bunnies twirl in a dust-up romance.

Beneath the fridge lies a lost fork's quest,
While spoons tell tales of the very best.
They chat about feasts and the grand designs,
In the festival of crumbs, they sip on sweet wines.

Each twilight brings mischief anew,
As shadows take form in a merry old brew.
So peek in the corners, don't be afraid,
For humor in hiding is aptly displayed.

Fables of the Forgotten

An old teddy bear with a button for eye,
Roots for adventure, though dusty and shy.
He rides on the back of a curious dog,
Who sniffs out the tales in the soft, hazy fog.

In the attic, a clock ticks a merry old tune,
It dances with shadows beneath the full moon.
Cobbwebs swirl like a party's confetti,
While time just giggles, feeling all setty.

A bookshelf mocks with its secrets untold,
Of whispered romances and legends of old.
Books might rustle, just to ignite,
The joy of a tale hidden from sight.

So grab yourself snacks, don't be a bore,
And listen to whispers from ceiling to floor.
For amidst all the dust, there's laughter a-plenty,
In fables unspoken, their joy never empty.

Legends Lurking in the Dark

In the corners, a world waits to play,
Where shadows concoct their mischievous ballet.
A squirrel in slippers, moonwalks the night,
Donning a hat that's absurdly tight.

The fridge hums a tune, all secrets it keeps,
While broccoli dreams of climbing in heaps.
Leftovers gossip about culinary fame,
As they plot a comeback, oh what a game!

A broom in the corner spins tales of the past,
Of cleaning adventures that never quite last.
Dust settles thick, but with humor and cheer,
These legends make merry, making dust disappear.

So next time you're alone in the night's velvet cloak,
Heed those legendary whispers and jests they evoke.
For lurking in darkness, the fun's just begun,
A world full of laughter, inviting us to run.

Looming Twilight Tales

In a town where whispers roam,
Cats wear hats, they call it home.
Wizards brew their teas with flair,
And elves dance lightly in the air.

The clock strikes twelve, the frogs all sigh,
Witches giggle as they fly high.
A pumpkin coach rolls down the lane,
While pumpkin pies chatter once again.

Through the mist, a ghostly chase,
With silly grins, they race in place.
The moonlight glimmers, laughs ignite,
In realms where mischief brims with light.

With shadows spinning jokes untold,
The secrets 'neath the night unfold.
So grab your friend, let laughter swell,
For in this twilight, all is well.

The Quiet Veil of Secrets

Behind a curtain, a shadow peeks,
A squirrel dressed up in polka streaks.
He juggles nuts with quite a flair,
While talking to a golden bear.

At dusk, the pogo sticks arise,
With goblins bouncing toward the skies.
They pop balloons with silly sounds,
And play tag, weaving 'round and 'round.

A gnome's got jokes, a knock-knock tale,
While pixies dance, their skirts a-frail.
The lanterns giggle, flickering light,
As crickets perform in the cool night.

Secrets whispered in the breeze,
Make even the grumpiest laugh with ease.
So come, dear friend, join this delight,
Where quiet veils spark fun at night.

Chronicles in the Shade

In the shade, where shadows creep,
Rabbits plot and crickets leap.
A snail's slow dance is quite absurd,
As he twirls around, not saying a word.

A hiccup from a sleeping bear,
Wakes up the chattering birds in mid-air.
The glowworms giggle, lighting the way,
While frogs in tuxedos join the fray.

A wise old owl shrieks with delight,
Telling tales of a feathery flight.
Each tale's more funny than the last,
In this realm where time spins fast.

So gather 'round, come take a seat,
In the shade where laughter greets.
These chronicles, both quirky and bold,
Unfold the magic, let your heart be told.

The Tapestry of Night

Under stars, where giggles blend,
The night unveils a comic trend.
With spiders weaving webs so fine,
And moths that dance in silly line.

A dragon sneezes, puffs of air,
While chasing fireflies without a care.
The moon plays cards with the rattling wind,
Laughs echo, as new tricks begin.

In every corner, shadows play,
A merry band making night their day.
With every twinkle, humor spreads,
As giggling shadows hop from beds.

So wrap yourself in this delight,
For laughter sparkles in the night.
The tapestry of fun is spun,
With threads of joy, it's just begun!

Ancestral Shadows

In the attic, once so dreary,
A box of clothes, all a bit leery.
A grandpa's hat, so oversized,
Makes me wonder, was he disguised?

Old photographs tell no lies,
Yet Uncle Bob's face makes me cry.
His mustache was grand, his fashion, a shock,
Was he a spy? Or just a bad clock?

A great-aunt's wig, with sequins galore,
Dancing in daylight, oh what a chore!
She twirled and spun, with elegance rare,
Yet tripped on her cat, did she care?

Each shadow whispers a comical plight,
Of family feuds turned to laughs every night.
With all their quirks, they lighten my heart,
In ancestral shadows, we all play a part.

Half-Told Legends

Around the fire, tall tales arise,
Of a rooster who could mesmerize.
He crowed at midnight, oh what a sight,
His rival, the owl, gave a frantic fright.

A fisherman, brave, with no fear of wet,
Said he once caught a fish, forget what he met.
With fins that could dance and a tail full of glee,
He swore on his life it was just like a spree.

In shadows of laughter, the tales interlace,
Of a ghost who misplaced his own face.
He searched near the fridge, near the swing, near the tree,
"Oh, where did it go? It was so good to see!"

A hero once tripped on his own bravado,
While rescuing kittens, his hat said "Cameo."
Half-told legends, so silly and bright,
Bring giggles and snickers, pure delight.

The Dark Enclave

In a town where shadows play hide and seek,
There's a secret club, but it's rather bleak.
With skeletons dancing, and ghosts on parade,
It's really just kids, in a spooky charade.

Their leader, a cat with a monocle too,
Claims 'witches and wizards' enjoy this view.
A broomstick with squeaks, it makes them all chuckle,
While they gather around for a game of huddle.

In the depths of the hall, there's a table to feast,
On cookies shaped like bats, no fear of the beast.
With chocolate eyeballs, they nibble with care,
In a dark enclave, full of giggle-filled air.

But beware of the mouse, who's the true surprise,
With a cape made of cheese, he enchants with his eyes.
The dark might be spooky, but here it's a blast,
In their quirky clubhouse, where shadows are cast.

Faint Traces of Yesteryear

In the attic, dust dances with glee,
Faint traces of memories whisper to me.
A typewriter clicks, though no one's in sight,
Typing out nonsense, late into the night.

Old shoes with stories, can barely stand tall,
Once dressed up for parties, now they're just small.
"Oh, were we cool? Did we ever have flair?"
In shadows, they giggle, "Do we even care?"

A clock that won't tick, but laughs like a fool,
Says "Time's just a concept; I prefer school!"
With faint traces left behind in the dust,
Comedic echoes fulfill all our trust.

So we gather these whispers, embrace what they say,
From yesteryear's shadows, they brighten the day.
Through laughs and through giggles, old tales come alive,

In a world where the past and the present all thrive.

Heed the Calls of the Night

The moonlight giggles, a bright surprise,
While owls play poker in clever disguise.
A raccoon winks, in a top hat so fine,
He deals out the cards, and they all sip on wine.

The crickets chirp with a jiving beat,
While fireflies dance on the warm, soft street.
A cat on a fence, making quite a scene,
Declares he's the ruler—where has he been?

An echoing laugh from a shadowed nook,
A ghost tells a joke; it's a real page-turner book.
But who really knows? It's all just for fun,
As the night whispers secrets, 'til daylight is done.

So heed the calls, let your spirit run free,
In the nightly antics, find joy, can't you see?
With laughter and whimsy, the shadows will play,
As the mischief unfolds, in a wild, cheesy way.

Visions Beneath the Surface

Beneath the calm, where the bubbles bloom,
A fish wears a glasses and checks for some gloom.
He whispers to turtles, 'Let's plan a big bash!'
And they giggle together, as they dive with a splash.

The octopus juggles, eight arms in the air,
A seaweed curtain—this party is rare!
The crabs grab the snacks, while they cut quite the rug,
They click their pincers, in a rhythm so snug.

The starfish come twirling, with flippers that glow,
And the angler fish flicks on his dazzling show.
With laughter aplenty, the deep sea's alive,
In visions so silly, where sea creatures thrive.

So dive in the depths, let the merriment flow,
In the splash of the waves, feel the joy overflow.
For beneath the surface, a world filled with cheer,
Awaits every creature, every swimmer near.

Stories in Shadows' Embrace

In the corners of dusk, where giggles reside,
A shadow swings by, and it dances with pride.
With a hat made of starlight, it winks and it twirls,
Counting the chuckles of soft-spoken swirls.

A lantern bug buzzes, with sass in its flight,
It spins tales of mischief under soft moonlight.
The darkness, a canvas for dreams dancing free,
A parade of the silly, come see, come and see!

A cat in a cape struts with charming flair,
While a dog in a tutu leaps high in the air.
The shadows all giggle, as they tumble and play,
Casting reflections of fun, come what may.

In the embrace of the night, let the laughter ignite,
For the world is a stage, when the stars shine so bright.
With shadows as friends, join the whimsical race,
As the night invents stories in its gentle embrace.

Underneath the Canopy

Underneath the canopy, where big leaves meet,
A squirrel spins tales, as he nibbles a treat.
His friends gather 'round for a nutty old yarn,
With a punch line so cheesy, it causes a charm.

The rabbits tap dance on the soft, mossy ground,
While the owls clap their wings, oh, what a sound!
A fox in a tuxedo shakes hands with the trees,
While a hedgehog sings in the light summer breeze.

The night wears a crown of stars glowing bright,
As the canopy rustles with whispers of light.
The laughter blends softly with crickets on cue,
In a magical forest, full of wonderful view.

So come sing and dance, revel in glee,
Underneath the canopy, wild and carefree.
For in this embrace of nature's delight,
The tales are all spun, in the heart of the night.

Interludes from the Abyss

In the depths, where the giggles creep,
Monsters dance while shadows sleep.
Their socks mismatched, a sight so rare,
Whispering tales of vanished hair.

A ghost with a hat made of cheese,
Juggles pickles, if you please.
With every slip, he makes a call,
To all the creatures in the hall.

The spider spins a web of fun,
Catching laughs instead of sun.
Tickling toes of the brave and bold,
A comedy show in the dark unfolds.

With a wink, the owl hoots a rhyme,
Embedding chuckles in the grime.
As moonlight drips like melted cream,
What a whimsical, laugh-filled dream!

Unwritten in the Dimness

In the corners where shadows play,
Twisted tales, they come out to stay.
A lamp that flickers with no light,
Tells hilarious jokes in the night.

A cat wearing spectacles, you see,
Tries to read but just shouts 'meow!' in glee.
With every fall, he leaps with style,
Chasing his tail for quite a while.

The broomsticks having a dance-off, oh!
A simple broom called 'Bobby' stole the show.
With each twirl, the dust turns to cheer,
Echoes of laughter, vibrant and clear.

In the quiet, absurdity flows,
Laughter bounces where nobody goes.
Every giggle hides a daring feat,
In the dark, where silliness meets.

Parables of the Obscured

At dusk, when the giggles entwine,
Lights turn out, but the laughter shines.
A troll baking cookies, what a surprise,
With icing that glows and rocky pies.

The fairies wear hats made of moss,
They argue about who should floss.
With glee, they chatter, throw sprinkles around,
Creating a grin from darkness profound.

A raccoon, dapper in a bow tie,
Recites poems to the stars up high.
His audience? Just a tree that sways,
While the moon nods along and plays.

In this realm, where shadows reside,
Laughter blooms, takes us for a ride.
Every whimsy has its playful twist,
As night drapes its cloak, we can't resist!

Forgotten Voices of the Night

In corners shadowed, whispers jest,
A ghost hosting a pillow fight fest.
With feathers flying, they cackle loud,
While daylight dreams of a sleepy shroud.

An old suitcase filled with missed chance,
Holds a teddy bear that loves to dance.
With a tap and a spin, he takes the floor,
As shadows gather, they beg for more.

Monsters share tales over bowls of soup,
Each spoonful comes with a giggling whoop.
With every slurp, they raise a cheer,
Reminding us laughter conquers fear.

Beneath the stars, where mischief hides,
The night unveils its jester vibes.
In every quiet nook, a chuckle awaits,
As forgotten voices share silly debates.

Voices from the Abyss

In the dark, there's a giggle,
A ghost with a trick up its sleeve.
It dances around with a wiggle,
Making shadows believe.

A cat in a top hat appears,
Declaring it's time for a show.
With jokes that will bring you to tears,
The darkness begins to glow.

Echoes of laughter resound,
From phantoms with puns on their mind.
In the gloom, joy can be found,
If you leave all the fear behind.

Then comes along the big boo,
Who tries to out-joke the rest.
With each quip and hilarious cue,
It's hard to tell who's the best.

Chronicles of the Concealed

In a cupboard, secrets are stored,
With socks that have traveled too far.
Each tale leaves the specter floored,
As they sip on a pickle jar.

The whispers of socks come alive,
Each one a comedian lost.
They plot and they plan to contrive,
Fun games that will never exhaust.

A left shoe gets into a spat,
With the right, it just cannot cope.
While slippers hold court, where they chat,
About all of their dreams and hope.

From deep in the quilt, they giggle,
Pillow fights break out with a dash.
Every poke and poke brings a wiggle,
In this laughter-filled, hidden bash.

Myths Among the Murmurs

Beneath the bed, tales intertwine,
With critters that chuckle with glee.
A spider spins yarns so divine,
Of places you'd never believe.

The shadowy figures play tricks,
Each one with its own little rhyme.
With giggles that do clever flicks,
They change the course of time.

One ghost swears it met a great king,
While the other just floats and eats cheese.
Such legends come forth in a swing,
In the hush, they do as they please.

Then, who could forget the brave bat,
Who wears tiny glasses and grins?
It shares jokes while flying in chat,
Collecting the giggles like wins.

Haunting Histories

Once there was a ghost quite silly,
Who loved to play tricks with a broom.
It sweeped and it scooped with a frilly,
Twirled dust while it danced in the gloom.

From the attic, came whispers of cheer,
Of tales where the spatula trips.
With every clang, laughter draws near,
As the kitchen does twirl and flips.

The tales told by curtains that sway,
Of spoons that have waltzed on the floor.
With every giggle, they'd sway and play,
As shadows joined in for encore.

In corners, the chuckles erupt,
With every new tale, there's delight.
Hauntingly funny and corrupt,
A comedy show every night.

Secrets Nestled in Nooks

In a corner so tight, a cat found a shoe,
Filled with old socks and a bit of fondue.
Whispers of mice in a giggly retreat,
Dancing around crumbs that were once a treat.

An old toy soldier claims he's the king,
But his subjects just laugh, oh, what a funny thing!
They gather for meetings at a quarter to four,
Discussing the cheese that they can't ignore.

The clock on the wall ticks in not-so-straight lines,
Its rhythm confuses the old warning signs.
And the dust bunnies play hide and seek games,
Rooting for laughter, calling out names.

So sneak into corners, take a moment to look,
For nooks have great tales that are not in a book.
Each giggle and whisper, a tale to bestow,
In places we often just glance over slow.

Beneath the Veil

Under old blankets, the ghosts gather round,
Sharing their secrets without making a sound.
The one in a top hat insists he's a star,
Though the popcorn spilled tells us just where they are.

A poltergeist dances with socks in a spin,
While a chandelier giggles, letting the fun in.
The shadows hold laughter, not chilling despair,
As they conspire to pull pranks for the pair.

Who knew that a ghost could pull off such tricks,
Making shadows do somersaults with a flick?
Beneath the veil, humor quietly creeps,
Turning dark corners into chuckling leaps.

With whispers of mischief and laughter so light,
The spooky old house feels merry tonight.
So next time it's quiet, do take a chance,
And join in the shenanigans that make you dance.

Dim Lighthouses of Lore

There once was a lighthouse, too dim for its trade,
Its light flickered off, like a plans badly made.
The keeper would laugh as he brewed up a tea,
In hopes the lost sailors would just take a spree.

With jellyfish picnics and crabs in a band,
The tunes they all played were not quite so grand.
Yet each passing wave would tap out a beat,
As the lighthouse swayed to the rhythm of heat.

Old barnacles played with the seabirds at dusk,
Plotting out schemes in the salty sea rust.
As gulls squawk with laughter at choices they make,
The lighthouse joins in, raising tall cups of cake.

So when you sail by, give a wave and a cheer,
For dim lighthouses keep the jests ever near.
In their glow, strange stories take flight and abound,
With myths that rise higher than the sea's salty sound.

Faint Glimmers of Forgotten Truths

In a dusty old attic, the whispers arise,
Where secrets and trinkets both giggle and sigh.
A hat that once traveled on a cat of great fame,
Recalls all the mischief it played with a name.

A mirror reflects jokes only it can understand,
With shadows of smiles played on its glassy land.
Each laugh that it captures spins tales quite absurd,
As whispers flit by, not a word left unheard.

With faint glimmers flashing, a glow up above,
The old table winks with its stories of love.
And the closet, though wise, cannot keep its cool,
As socks form a band, declaring it's a rule!

So unfold the old quilts, let the laughter unwind,
For every old corner has treasures to find.
In glimmers of laughter, old truths still ignite,
Bringing humor to shadows, lighting up the night.

Forgotten Voices of Dawn

In the morning mist, I hear a tale,
Of socks and shoes that lost their sail.
A cat in pajamas wrote a book,
With pages of fish and a friendly rook.

The rooster crows at his sleepy friend,
Who snoozes on the couch till the very end.
The sun says hello with a giggle and gleam,
As shadows dance in a wobbly dream.

A baker's loaf starts to run away,
Chased by crumbs in a silly play.
They twirl and leap, what a funny sight,
Creating laughter till the fall of night.

With every hue of dawn's bright art,
Forgotten voices sing from the heart.
They tickle the air with whispers of mirth,
A joyful reminder of the day's rebirth.

Lanterns in the Abyss

Deep in the dark where giggles reside,
Lanterns glow with a curious pride.
They flicker and flirt with shadows nearby,
Making faces that giggle and sigh.

A fish on a bike zips past in a flash,
Chasing its tail in an underwater dash.
The octopus grins with ice cream in hand,
Serving up cones in this weird, wacky land.

As whispers float from the depths of the night,
A frog on a lily leaps with delight.
He croaks out a song in the moon's playful light,
Turning lanterns into stars of the night.

In the abyss where laughter reigns,
The echoes of joy break all the chains.
A whimsical dance in the deep, dark sea,
Brings to life the lanterns, wild and free.

Mystique of the Shadows

In the corners where silliness lurks,
Shadows whisper their playful quirks.
A wizard with glasses makes jokes with a broom,
Casting spells that cause flowers to bloom.

A raccoon in a hat strums on a tune,
While turtles in shades dance under the moon.
They twirl with glee, what a comical sight,
As shadows join in with sheer delight.

The ghouls and the goblins are up to some fun,
Trading their tricks in a turn of the sun.
With laughter echoing through the trees,
They scare away gloom with the greatest of ease.

Beneath the twinkling stars' gentle glow,
Mystique wraps the night, as soft breezes blow.
In shadowy realms where the whimsical play,
Laughter endures till the break of day.

Silhouettes in the Silence

In the hush of the night, silhouettes prance,
A lively crew caught in a moonlit dance.
With one cheeky monkey, they spin and sway,
Chasing their shadows until break of day.

An elephant wearing a bright polka-dot dress,
Sways to a rhythm that's anyone's guess.
While lions that giggle play hide and seek,
Beneath the soft glow, the silence feels chic.

A penguin in tuxedo joins in the game,
Sliding on ice with a wild claim to fame.
They tumble and laugh 'till the sun begins to rise,
As chuckles and squeaks fill the starlit skies.

Silhouettes shimmer in the calm and hush,
Creating a ruckus, in their fun little crush.
In the quiet of night, their joy takes flight,
Filling the silence with laughter so bright.

Echoes of the Lost

In corners where the dust bunnies play,
Old socks and keys lose their way.
A pizza slice left out for days,
Whispers of laughter in strange arrays.

The cat with a secret, perched on a chair,
Eyes glinting with mischief, a wink and a stare.
Chasing shadows that dart and flare,
While we wonder just what is there.

Beneath the bed lies a treasure map,
Leading to crumbs and a half-eaten flap.
Monsters giggle, a soft clapping clap,
As we search for the source of the mishap.

So here we sit, in our own silly plight,
Sharing giggles with ghosts of the night.
In hallways filled with joy and fright,
Echoes of lost things take flight.

Lurkers at the Edge of Dreams

At the cusp where the daylight fades,
A squirrel in pajamas prances in spades.
He steals the last cookie—oh, the charades!
While our dreams are being played in parades.

A shadowy figure in a fluffy disguise,
Well, that's just my dog with his mischief-prize.
He naps as he guards all the bright fireflies,
And giggles at sleep with his sleepy eyes.

The clock ticks a tune, a comical clock,
That dances and sings with every tick-tock.
Each second a giggle, a slip, and a shock,
Where fun proportions go round like a rock.

So when you drift off, don't be surprised,
By laughter from corners that seem disguised.
With lurkers of whimsy, you'll find the prize,
In dreams where the silliness never dies.

Narratives in the Night

In the quiet of night, the owls take flight,
Telling tales that twist and delight.
A raccoon in a top hat joins in sight,
As they plot mischief till morning light.

The moon whispers jokes to the clouds up high,
While stars scribble punchlines in the sky.
A hedgehog recites with a gleam in his eye,
A tale of his quest for a pizza pie.

Giggles arise from the thickets and trees,
A chorus of laughter floats on the breeze.
With crickets performing as comic dear tease,
They weave silly tales with effortless ease.

So as you lay down, take heed of the night,
With narratives sprouting and taking flight.
Embrace the silly, and hold on tight,
For joy often finds us when dreams feel right.

Chronicles of the Invisible

A sock puppet army in the laundry swirl,
In battles with lint, they twirl and whirl.
Invisible knights in a cotton-tied hurl,
Duel with the dryer, like a bright pearl.

The vacuum hums tales of daring feats,
Against crumbs and dust, how it bravely defeats.
While behind the couch, a mouse discreet,
Giggles at quests, like little elites.

A calendar filled with epic quests,
Planned out adventures for all the best rests.
But forgetting the plans leads to jesting tests,
And chasing lost dreams, oh what a fest!

So raise a toast to the hidden and bold,
In chronicles where the unseen unfolds.
For laughter resides where we're often sold,
The magic that's real, yet never told.

The Underbelly of Time

In a clock that ticks backward, I found a lost cat,
Wearing a top hat, he squawked, 'Ain't life a spat?'
With a wink and a grin, he danced on a dime,
Claiming he could outrun the hands of time.

The dog in the corner just laughed with delight,
'You think you're the fastest? Oh, what a sight!'
They traded old tales of who stole the cheese,
And giggled together, so light on the breeze.

A pair of old shoes whispered juicy gossip,
'You won't believe who ran off with a mop!'
The cat purred and nodded, 'I knew it all along,
The truth is much funnier, hidden in song.'

So beneath all the laughter, where truths start to blend,
Time spun its web and invited a friend,
With a chuckle and jape, life took a new turn,
In the underbelly, where shadows all burn.

Obscured Truths

Under the floorboards, a squirrel sits tight,
With secrets aplenty, oh what a fright!
He munches on acorns and cackles with glee,
'You'll never believe just who visits me!'

A ghost took a dip in the old bathtub,
Wearing a towel, he made quite a hubbub,
'It's not easy haunting, you know, it's a grind,
But free soap and shampoo? Now that's something kind!'

Behind every curtain, a specter drags tales,
Of picnic disasters or failed giant snails,
The laughter erupts as truths slip away,
In the land of the lost, no one cares what they say.

So gather your whispers, your giggles and pranks,
In the dance of obscured, let's fill up our ranks,
With tales that are twisted, but oh so sincere,
In the juggling shadows, let's drink up the cheer!

Hushed Whispers of the Past

In a dusty drawer lived a sock on the run,
Its mate in a battle, they always had fun,
'Why did I cross the road?' it chuckled, bemused,
'For the chicken I chased, now I'm totally confused!'

The wallpaper sighed, recounting its wear,
'What was that stain? Oh dear, I must share!'
Laughter erupted from cracks in the floor,
'At least I'm not decorated with last night's galore!'

Along came a teapot, pouring tales of tea,
'In the days of old, I was someone of glee,
But now, in this kitchen, I'm stuck with a clatter,
Of idle young spoons, who just chitchat and chatter!'

So hush all your worries, let the past have its say,
In the cloak of old whispers, we'll dance and we'll play,
For time may conceal what we think is the truth,
But laughter's the remedy, preserving our youth.

Unfolding Tales in Darkness

Under the bed, where the dust bunnies plot,
A wily old sock once lived with a lot,
'We'll scheme and we'll dream of the world soft and wide,

While humans sleep soundly, we'll go for a ride!'

Each night they would wander, slipping through cracks,
Sneaking past shoes and avoiding the snacks,
Giggles exploded in the shadowy halls,
As they fashioned their plans while avoiding falls.

In a closet, a coat began telling tall tales,
Of the winters it faced and its adventurous trails,
It laughed about puddles that soaked all its seams,
While the shoes on the shelf planned for their dreams.

So embrace all the shadows where funny tales play,
In the dark, there's a laughter that brightens the sway,
For life's an adventure, hidden in night,
And the unfolding of tales makes the heart feel so light.

Tread Softly Upon the Dark

Beneath the moon's mischievous grin,
Where shadows dance and giggles begin.
A ghost trips over a garden gnome,
And suddenly feels far from home.

The owl hoots, giving a cheeky wink,
As the bats play tag, making us think.
A cat in a top hat struts with flair,
Saying, 'Join my ball, if you dare!'

The trees whisper secrets, just for fun,
While squirrels debate who's fastest to run.
A witch loses her spell, makes a pie fly,
Leaving a trail of laughter in the sky.

So tread softly, but don't hold your breath,
For in this dark, there's always a jest.
With shadows as friends, join in the prance,
For who knew the dark could dance so enhanced?

Folklore from the Whispering Haze

In the mist, there's a tale most silly,
Of three-legged frogs that dance near the willy.
They croak funny limericks, oh what a sight,
Making the crickets crack up with delight.

A lost sock floats by with a grin so wide,
Singing about its adventurous ride.
It figured the washing machine was a trip,
Where socks must go to learn how to flip.

A spooky old tree offers tricks with treats,
It steals your sandwich, swaps in some beets.
With roots that wiggle and branches that sway,
It tells knock-knock jokes that brighten the day.

So laugh with the shadows, let worries pass,
For in the misty night, all is in sass.
Whisper your wishes, let laughter amaze,
And dance in the glow of the moon's gentle blaze.

Dances of the Nightshade

The nightshade blooms in whimsical cheer,
With petals that giggle and buzz in your ear.
A beetle in ballet shoes twirls around,
While fireflies flash the best light show in town.

A raccoon hosts a critique on the moon,
Debating its brightness with a funny tune.
Each night they gather, a sight to behold,
With laughter that echoes like tales of old.

The shadows play games of hide and seek,
While owls make puns — oh, aren't they unique?
And bats wear bow ties, oh what a scene,
As they twirl through the air, so graceful and keen.

So join in the revelry, let spirits soar,
With nightshade delights and laughter galore.
For in the heart of the dark, let's find our groove,
Dancing with shadows, we'll always improve.

Unseen Tales of the Twilight

Twilight whispers secrets, just for a laugh,
As tadpoles in tuxedos practice a craft.
They plot murky pranks, like hiding the moon,
While frogs play the violin—a lovely tune.

A rabbit with glasses reads tales from the dusk,
Winking at owls, inquiring, 'Is that musk?'
While raccoons bake cakes using raindrop juice,
And throw wild parties with no need for a truce.

The stars hang like pendants, so shiny and bright,
While shadows drink coffee — oh what a sight!
With a wink and a nod, they share tales anew,
About mischief and marvels the unseen can do.

So linger with whimsy, let laughter ignite,
As unseen tales dance in the heart of the night.
In the twilight's embrace, we'll sing with delight,
For magic's alive when the day turns to night.

Lingering Footprints

A raccoon stole my sandwich, it's true,
Took a bite, then vanished from view.
I chased him down, but what a sight,
He waddled away, he's quite the light!

In the park, we play hide and seek,
Beneath the swings, I try not to peek.
But the laughter echoes, oh what a tease,
Even the squirrels dance with ease!

Each footprint tells a silly tale,
Of goofy stunts and wild, wind-filled sail.
With every stride, a chuckle grows,
In this place where mischief flows!

So here's to footprints, quirky and bold,
To the snickers and giggles, some stories retold.
Let's savor the laughs as we stomp the ground,
In this playful heart, joy is found!

Dimly Lit Chronicles

In a corner dark, a mouse held a feast,
He nibbled on crumbs, like a furry beast.
The candlelight flickered, casting a show,
As shadows danced to the tales of woe.

A ghost tried to scare, but slipped on a mat,
Tripped over the cat, now isn't that scat?
He mumbled, 'I just want to be frightful,'
But ended up looking quite delightful!

The old broomstick joined in with a groove,
Swirling 'round the room, trying to prove.
That even in darkness, there's fun to be found,
With giggles and chuckles, and joy going 'round!

So raise up a glass, let's toast to the night,
To the mischief and laughter, pure delight!
In dimly lit corners, we gather and cheer,
For all of the fun that brings us near!

Secrets of the Forgotten Grove

Amidst the trees, a parrot squawks loud,
Sharing secrets, he feels quite proud.
He whispers of hidden treasures so rare,
But mostly just brags about his hair!

The fox tells tales of the last critter race,
Where the turtles lost by a snail's pace.
A rabbit jumped high, claiming first place,
But slipped on a berry—what a comical face!

A squirrel emerges with acorns to sell,
Saying, 'Buy one, get one! It's a great deal!'
With each nut he sells, he winks with glee,
As a dancing raccoon joins in, quite free!

In the grove, there's magic and silliness found,
With laughter echoing throughout the ground.
So let's gather 'round, share in our tales,
In the secrets of laughter, joy never fails!

In the Quiet Between

In the moments of hush, a snail made a plan,
To race against ants in a measured span.
They laughed and they squealed, 'Oh what a show!'
As the fastest of feet said, 'Just go slow!'

Beneath the soft leaves, a secret was found,
A rock whispered jokes that bounced all around.
The mushrooms all giggled, their caps bobbing high,
As the owl clapped his wings, letting out a sigh.

A faint breeze carried the chuckles of trees,
As they swayed side to side with the greatest of ease.
The shadows played games, in a soft, gentle way,
Turning everything funny, come night or day!

So in the quiet, let's cheer and delight,
For laughter and joy make the world feel just right.
Between every whisper, a chuckle will bloom,
In the secrets of silence, there's always room!

www.ingramcontent.com/pod-product-compliance
Lightning Source LLC
Chambersburg PA
CBHW071851160426
43209CB00003B/508